POCKET GUIDE TO
The Night Sky

BRIAN JONES

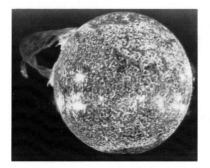

POCKET GUIDE TO
The Night Sky

BRIAN JONES

CRESCENT BOOKS
New York • Avenel, New Jersey

©1992 Salamander Books Ltd.,
129-137 York Way,
London N7 9LG,
United Kingdom.

This 1993 edition published by Crescent Books,
distributed by Outlet Book Company, Inc.,
a Random House Company, 40 Engelhard Avenue,
Avenel, New Jersey 07001

ISBN 0-517-08644-1

8 7 6 5 4 3 2 1

Credits

Editor: Chris Westhorp
Designer: Paul Johnson
Charts: Brian Jones & Paul Johnson
Filmset: The Old Mill, London

Color reproduction: P&W Graphics PTE Ltd, Singapore
Printed in Belgium by Proost International Book Production

The Author
Brian Jones is an astronomy and spaceflight writer-
broadcaster based in Yorkshire, northern England.
He has written a dozen books on the subject and worked
on numerous collaborations such as the *Children's
Britannica Yearbook*. He has also been on television and
radio on a number of occasions.

Picture credits
All pictures were supplied by Starland Picture Library.
The copyright holders are as follows: Bernard Abrams,
page 54; Aerospatiale, 7 (top right); Anglo-Australian
Telescope Board, 53 (left); European Space Agency, 7
(top right), 23, 33; ESO, 32 (left), 48, 58, 60; Chris Floyd,
39, 43 (right), 63, (left); FAS, 14 (bottom), 26, 28, 31
(right), 34, 40, 42; Raymond Livori, 42; Lowell
Observatory, 22; National Optical Astronomy
Observatories, 24, 25, 29, 30, 31 (left), 32 (right), 46, 50,
63 (right); National Aeronautics & Space Administration,
8, 9, 10, 11, 12, 13, 14 (top), 15, 16, 17, 18, 19, 20, 21; Ken
Philips, 34; Royal Observatory, Edinburgh, 44, 45, 53
(left), 56, 62; Andrew Sefton, 26; Colin Taylor, 28, 40; Bob
Tuffnel, 15 (bottom), 31 (right); Yerkes Observatory, 6, 7
(bottom left), 27, 52; University of Chicago, 6.

Contents

	Page
INTRODUCTION	6
THE SOLAR SYSTEM	8
THE SUN	10
THE MOON	12
MERCURY AND VENUS	14
MARS	16
JUPITER AND SATURN	18
URANUS AND NEPTUNE	20
PLUTO AND CHARON	22
COMETS	24
METEORS AND METEORITES	26
AURORAE	28
STELLAR EVOLUTION	30
THE STARS	34
THE NORTH CIRCUMPOLAR STARS	40
THE ORION TO ERIDANUS REGION	42
THE LYNX TO PUPPIS REGION	46
THE LEO, VIRGO AND HYDRA REGIONS	48
THE HERCULES TO SCORPIUS REGION	50
THE SUMMER TRIANGLE	54
THE CAPRICORNUS TO SAGITTARIUS REGION	56
THE PEGASUS TO PISCIS AUSTRINUS REGION	58
THE SOUTH CIRCUMPOLAR STARS	60
INDEX	64

INTRODUCTION

Ever since the first stargazers looked up at the sky thousands of years ago, the stars have fascinated mankind. Hundreds of prehistoric structures still remain standing which were built using astronomical principles. These peoples had sacred animals and gods which they believed were revealed by the stars in the sky. Some of the mythologies which have developed are sophisticated and remain strongly held beliefs in many parts of the world.

Left: *A battle between Medes and Lydians on 28 May 585BC was brought to a halt by a nearly total solar eclipse. Seen by the Ancients as a sign from the Gods the eclipse was also special because it had been calculated accurately by Thales of Miletus who had studied the Sun before making his prediction.*

The first true astronomers to establish our modern roots were the Egyptians who, in around 3,000BC, gave us the 365-day calendar. The Egyptians also divided the stars into patterns, or constellations, and made accurate measurements of stellar positions.

From around 1,000BC Chinese and Indian astronomers observed many different celestial phenomena, including eclipses, comets, meteors and the motions of the Moon and planets. The Chinese also drew up constellations, as did the Babylonians and Greeks who identified 48 of them (including the 12 of the Zodiac). The birth of Thales of Miletus in 624BC marked the dawn of the Greek era, and from then until the death of Ptolemy in AD 180 our understanding of the sky advanced remarkably.

Although several Greek astronomers believed the Earth and planets orbited the Sun, the Earth was generally thought to be situated at the centre of the Universe, with the Sun, Moon and planets moving around it. Ptolemy, the last of the Greek astronomers, summarised this idea in his great book *Almagest*, and what became known as the Ptolemaic Theory held sway for many centuries.

In 1543 the Polish astronomer Nicolas Copernicus advanced the idea that the Earth was one of a number of planets travelling around the Sun in circular orbits. His work paved the way for a revolution in astronomy. A German mathematician and astronomer, Johannes Kepler, improved upon the Copernican Theory and offered proof that the Earth did indeed orbit the Sun.

Kepler was assistant to the Danish astronomer Tycho Brahe, a firm believer in the Ptolemaic Theory. Kepler studied Brahe's observations and concluded that the planets did indeed move around the Sun. However, their orbits were not circular but elliptical. Their distances from the Sun varied, thus explaining the discrepancies between the Copernican Theory and the observed motions of the planets. Kepler's work finally established order and lay the foundations for future astronomers to expand our knowledge of the Universe.

Following the invention of the telescope in 1608, the Italian astronomer Galileo Galilei became one of the first to carry out telescopic observations of the sky. He made many discoveries, including the fact that the pearly band of the Milky Way was in fact comprised of the light from many millions of individual stars.

Telescopes have allowed us to expand our knowledge of the Universe greatly and make remarkable discoveries. Today, telescopes of incredible size and ability allow astronomers to probe the Universe as never before. The launch of the Hubble Space Telescope in 1990 led to astronomers being

Right: *Scientists examining the Infra-Red Astronomy Satellite prior to its launch in 1983. A great deal of energy comes to us from Space but much of it is blocked by our atmosphere, thus the detectors are put into Earth orbit in order to study the full spectrum.*

able to peer out at the Universe from Earth orbit, giving us our clearest views yet.

Perhaps even more exciting are the probes, satellites and manned space missions. Currently, NASA's Galileo probe is heading for Jupiter to survey the giant planet and its moons.

Studies of energy reaching us from the sky have also yielded much information. The Infra-Red Astronomy Satellite (IRAS), launched in 1983, was very useful. More recently, the Cosmic Background Explorer (COBE) made dramatic discoveries about the creation of the Universe itself. Many others are currently operated or planned.

The future holds more missions: NASA's Comet Rendezvous and Asteroid Flyby is due to launch in 1995; a polar lunar orbiter may be launched; and a Mars Observer spacecraft is also planned. Mankind's journey into the stars is only just at the beginning.

Left: *Copernicus whose mistake was to think the planets orbited the sun in perfect circles.*

Right: *Galileo was forced by the church to retract his "heretical" views.*

THE SOLAR SYSTEM

The Solar System comprises the Sun, planets and their satellites, comets, meteoroids and interplanetary material. The way that this is distributed gives us clues as to how the Solar System originated. For example, the four inner, terrestrial planets are all small, rocky objects while the four outer planets are all gaseous in composition. By studying this and other evidence, astronomers have pieced together a theory of how the Sun and planets came into being.

The Solar System formed from a rotating cloud of gas and dust known as the solar nebula, the rotation eventually leading to its flattening out into a disc. Most of the heavier elements within the solar nebula collected together in the central regions of the cloud through the actions of gravity. This produced a

Planetary Data

Planet	Diameter (km)	Distance from Sun (km)	Sidereal period (Year)	Axial rotation period	Number of satellites
Mercury	4,880	58,000,000	87.97 days	58.65 days	0
Venus	12,104	108,000,000	224.7 days	243.01 days	0
Earth	12,756	149,600,000	365.26 days	23.93 hours	1
Mars	6,796	227,900,000	686.98 days	24h 37m 23s	2
Jupiter	143,800	778,300,000	11.86 years	9h 50m 30s	16
Saturn	120,660	1,427,000,000	29.46 years	10h 13m 59s	18
Uranus	50,800	2,870,000,000	84.01 years	17h 14m	15
Neptune	49,500	4,497,000,000	164.79 years	17h 50m	8
Pluto	2,300	5,900,000,000	24 years	6.3874 days	1

Note: The axial rotation period given here is that for the equatorial region.

Above: *This is a composite showing several planetary members of our Solar System. The belts, zones and Great Red Spot of mighty Jupiter are seen at top left; to the right is a Voyager 2 image of Neptune; at upper right is Saturn; in the centre is the Red Planet — Mars; and at lower left is cloud-covered Venus. The pride of place goes to our home planet as it was seen by the Apollo astronauts who rounded the Moon to be greeted by the sight of Earth rising above the lunar landscape.*

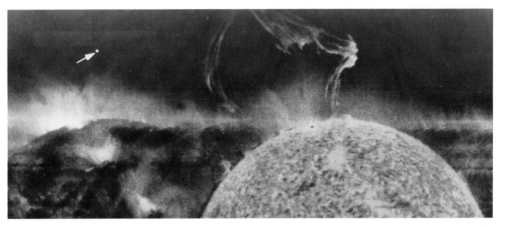

Right: *The power of solar activity can be appreciated in this Skylab photograph of a huge eruption leaving the Sun's surface. The scale of this event can be judged by comparing with the size of the arrowed white dot which is scaled to represent Earth. It is a sobering thought that the Sun is a very ordinary star.*

shift of mass towards the centre of the solar nebula and an increase in temperature, density and pressure in this region. A protostar was formed and temperatures and pressures at its core built up until a stage was reached whereby nuclear reactions commenced and the Sun began to shine.

Particles in the surrounding disc of material collected together to form the planets; the terrestrial ones formed from the heavier elements that had gathered together in the region of the protostar, the lighter elements in the outer regions of the disc (such as hydrogen and helium) went to form the gaseous planets.

Particles within the inner regions of the disc collided and remained together, eventually building up into small objects called planetesimals. The process of collision continued with the planetesimals colliding and sticking together to form protoplanets, which in turn built up into today's planets.

The process was similar for the outer planets, although once the limited supply of heavier elements had run out the objects that were to form the rocky cores of the gaseous planets began to accumulate vast amounts of the gas that was abundant in the outer regions of the solar nebula. The available gas was gathered up to form hydrogen-rich atmospheres around the rocky cores, thereby creating the outer planets. Once the planets had formed, the constant force of the solar wind drove away any light elements that still remained in the vicinity of our star.

THE SUN

Although only an ordinary star the Sun is huge by terrestrial standards with a diameter of 110 times that of our planet. The close proximity of the Sun means that we can constantly monitor solar activity.

When we look at the Sun we gaze down on its outer visible surface, or photosphere. Yet the huge amounts of energy emitted by the Sun are generated not there, but at the Sun's core where the temperature is 15 million°C and the pressure equal to 340,000 times that of the atmosphere at the Earth's surface. These conditions give rise to nuclear reactions during which hydrogen nuclei are fused together to form the heavier element helium. A tiny amount of mass is left over from the reaction and this leaves the core and slowly makes its way to the photosphere from where it emerges as light and heat.

Sunspots
The best known solar features are sunspots. A typical sunspot has a dark central umbra surrounded by a lighter penumbra. The temperature of a sunspot umbra is around 3,800°C, considerably cooler than the surrounding photosphere. Sunspots

SUN DATA	
Equatorial diameter	: 1,392,000km
Surface temperature	: 5,500°C
Mass (Earth=1)	: 332,946
Volume (Earth=1)	: 1,303,600
Mean distance from Earth	: 149,597,900km (92,975,700 miles)

Above: *The pearly glow of the solar corona as seen from Miahuatlan, Mexico, during a total solar eclipse in March 1970.*

10

Above: *The solar corona's density, ranging from purple (densest) to yellow, is revealed in this image prepared from satellite data.*

only appear dark because they are so much cooler than the photosphere. This activity takes place over a period which averages out at 11 years. At times of minimum activity, the solar surface may be devoid of sunspots for weeks or even months on end, in total contrast to periods of maximum activity when huge numbers of spots can sometimes be seen.

Other Solar Activity

From the photosphere solar energy passes through a region called the chromosphere within which flares and faculae are seen. Flares are bright streamers of hot hydrogen. These short-lived but brilliant eruptions give off charged particles which may eventually reach the Earth and give rise to increased auroral activity. Faculae are highly luminous clouds of gas which often appear above areas where sunspots are about to form. The most energetic examples of solar activity, however, are undoubtedly prominences. Comprised mainly of hydrogen these huge columns of gas rise impressively from the solar surface in one of two basic forms: *quiescent* prominences are fairly stable and have often been observed to hang almost motionless above the solar surface for days on end; *eruptive* prominences, on the other hand, are huge masses of gas travelling away from the surface at speed.

The solar corona lies above the chromosphere. Reaching out to a distance of several million kilometres, the corona is the outer region of the Sun's atmosphere. Emerging from the corona is the solar wind, the constant flow of energized particles emitted by the Sun in all directions.

Solar Eclipses

Although the Sun is a great deal larger than the Moon, it is also much further away. As a result, the two objects have virtually the same apparent size when viewed from Earth. Solar eclipses take place when the Moon's orbit carries it between the Earth and Sun. If the alignment is exact a *total* eclipse will be seen with the lunar disc completely blotting out the Sun; *partial* eclipses occur if the alignment isn't exact and only part of the Sun is obscured.

THE MOON

The Moon is thought to have been formed long ago following the impact with Earth of an object roughly the size of Mars. The debris from the impacting body entered into Earth orbit, eventually collecting together to form the Moon.

Following its formation the Moon was bombarded by meteorites, thus creating the huge numbers of craters strewn across the lunar landscape. Dark material from beneath the

lunar surface then spilled out to fill the low-flying regions of the Moon and create the dark areas we see today.

These dark regions were once though to be expanses of water and were given names like Mare Serenitatis (Sea of Serenity), Pallus Nebularum (Marsh of Mists) and Oceanus Procellarum (Ocean of Storms). Today we know that there is no water on the lunar surface, although the names given to these features have been retained. Even a casual glance at the Moon will show the contrast between the dark maria and the much brighter cratered highland regions.

The Moon orbits Earth in the same time that it takes to rotate once on its axis; this means that the same lunar hemisphere faces us all the time. The Moon's orbit, however, is not exactly circular and its distance from us varies slightly. The orbital period and axial rotation period get slightly out of step with each other and the effect of this is that the Moon "wobbles" slightly from side to side. Known as libration, this sideways wobble allows us to see up to 59 per cent of the lunar surface over a period of time.

Manned Exploration
The Moon is the only other world upon which manned spacecraft have landed. In 1969 the American Apollo 11 mission touched down in Mare Tranquilitatis (Sea of Tranquillity). On board were Neil Armstrong and Edwin Aldrin

Left: *The large, dark area near the centre of this Apollo 10 photograph is Mare Tranquillitatis (The Sea of Tranquility).*

who became the first men to set foot on the Moon. Apollo 11 was followed by five more successful manned landings during the following three years and plans are now being made for a return to the Moon leading to the eventual setting up of a permanent manned lunar base. How budget cuts affect such plans remains to be seen.

Lunar Eclipses
A lunar eclipse occurs at full Moon when the Moon's orbit carries it into the Earth's shadow. The sunlight which normally illuminates the Moon is cut off and the lunar surface darkens considerably. If the Moon passes completely into the umbra a total lunar eclipse occurs; partial eclipses take place when only part of the Moon enters this region.

If the Moon only enters the penumbra of the Earth's shadow a penumbral eclipse takes place during which the darkening effect is only slight and difficult to observe.

Lunar eclipses do not occur every month because the Moon's orbit around the Earth is tilted relative to the orbital plane of the Earth around the Sun. It is only infrequently that the three bodies become aligned and an eclipse can occur. One will take place in mid-December 1992.

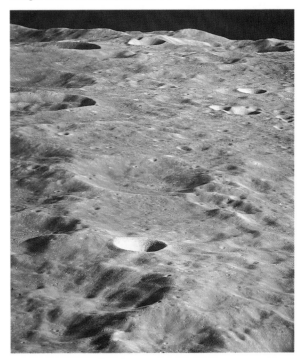

Below: *The rugged, crater-strewn landscape of the lunar farside as seen from astronauts aboard the Apollo 10 lunar module. There are thought to be about 500,000 craters on the Moon's surface.*

MOON DATA	
Equatorial diameter	: 3,476km (2,160 miles)
Axial rotation period	: 27.32 days
Orbital period	: 27.32 days
Mean distance from Earth	: 384,400km (238,906 miles)
Maximum distance from Earth	: 406,697km (252,764 miles)
Minimum distance from Earth	: 356,410km (221,510 miles)

MERCURY AND VENUS

Mercury

Because Mercury is the closest planet to the Sun it is always seen close to the Sun in the sky and is generally swamped by the Sun's glare. Earth-based astronomers had never managed successfully to observe the planet; then in 1974 and 1975 the American Mariner 10 space probe made three close fly-bys of the planet, its cameras providing us with our first clear views of its surface.

Mariner 10 gazed down upon a crater-strewn world, the smallest of them measuring approximately 100 metres (90 yards) across, with the largest, named "Beethoven", some 625km (388miles) in diameter. There are certainly many craters which were too small to be seen by Mariner 10. Other features imaged by the Mariner 10 cameras include mountains and valleys, ridges and cliffs — examples of the latter being seen to meander across the Mercurian surface.

The Mercurian surface is similar in many ways to that of the Moon, although there are very few of the flat, dark maria we see on the lunar surface. The largest feature spotted by Mariner 10 was the Caloris Basin, a huge impact feature some 1,300km (808miles) in diameter and surrounded by lofty mountain chains.

Internally, Mercury possesses a large iron core with a diameter of around 4,000km (2,500miles). Above this is a rocky crust with a depth of between 500 and 600km (300 and 375miles). Mercury's iron core, large in comparison to the planet itself, means that Mercury has more iron than any other planetary member of the Solar System.

Above: *Mariner 10's photo-mosaic of the mountainous boundary of the Caloris Basin. Some features tower 2km above the terrain.*

Left: *Venus (lower left) and Mercury as they can look to the naked eye at sunset.*

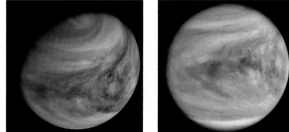

Above: *Left to right, an ultraviolet sequence over a 38-hour period which shows the clouds that revolve around Venus.*

Venus

Attempts to explore Venus through Earth-based telescopes have also proved unsuccessful, although for very different reasons. Venus is completely covered in dense white clouds which hide the surface completely from view. These clouds reflect nearly 80 per cent of the sunlight they receive back into space, making Venus the brightest of the planets.

Venus also has a thick, choking atmosphere which produces a surface atmospheric pressure 90 times that at the Earth's surface! The Venusian atmosphere is comprised mainly of carbon dioxide with various other gases present, including carbon monoxide and sulphur dioxide.

Carbon dioxide is a "greenhouse gas". It allows the heat from the Sun to reach the Venusian surface, but then traps it and prevents it escaping back into space. This has produced a Venusian surface temperature in excess of 450°C!

Astronomers have managed to observe the Venusian surface by the use of space probes. Soviet Venera probes have managed to land on the surface. As well as photographs, data received from these probes included information on atmospheric conditions and examination of soil samples.

The latest and most successful Venusian radar-mapper is the American Magellan probe. Radar mapping involves the beaming down through the clouds of radar pulses. These are reflected off the surface and back to the orbiting probe. The shorter the distance travelled by the pulse, the quicker it will return to the space probe. Radar pulses hitting valleys and other low-lying features would therefore take longer to come-back than those hitting mountains, crater walls and other highland areas.

Nearly all the Venusian surface has been mapped in this way and many features have been plotted including craters, mountains and possibly-active volcanoes. Most of the surface is flat, rolling plain although there are several large highland areas, notably Aphrodite Terra and Ishtar Terra.

MARS

The strong blood-red colour of Mars has led to it being named after the legendary Roman God of War. Often referred to as the Red Planet, its colouration is due to vast areas of reddish oxidized dust scattered across the Martian surface rather than temperature, for Mars is a cold, forbidding planet. It has two moons: Deimos (Terror) and Phobos (Fear).

Mars has long attracted the attentions of astronomers, not least because it was once thought to contain intelligent life. In 1877 the Italian astronomer Giovanni Schiaparelli turned his telescope towards Mars and noted a number of straight markings on its surface. He referred to these markings as "canali", a word which indicates naturally-occurring channels. Yet the word was translated incorrectly as "canals", which are anything but natural, and several astronomers then concluded that the surface of Mars was covered by a system of canals built by intelligent Martians to carry water from the planet's polar regions to the drier areas near the equator. It was not until space probes visited the planet and sent back photographs of its surface that this was finally disproved.

Space probes have revealed a fascinating world containing many craters and many other notable features. There are several huge volcanoes, including the gigantic Olympus Mons, a colossal feature towering 25km (15 miles) above the Martian plains. Olympus Mons measures over 600km (370 miles) across! Stretching away from the region of Olympus Mons and along the Martian equatorial region is Vallis Marineris, a huge valley system with a total length of around 4,000km (2,500 miles).

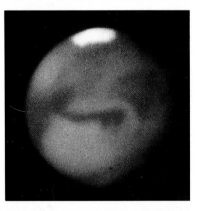

Right: *Both of Mars' ice caps can be seen here — one better than the other. They are a mixture of water ice and frozen CO_2.*

Below: *The first colour picture of the Martian surface taken by Viking 1 in July 1976 in the Chryse Planitia area.*

By far the most successful Mars' probes were the two American Vikings which landed on the surface in 1976. Many photographs were taken as well as data being collected on surface conditions, wind speeds, and temperatures and the analysing of soil samples. There were even attempts to detect life in the Martian soil although these were, at best, inconclusive. The results were beamed back to Earth via the two Viking orbiters which were travelling around Mars. The orbiters themselves took many thousands of pictures of Mars from high above its surface, helping scientists to chart the planet as never before. An ambitious joint project involving Russia, France and the USA is scheduled for launch in 1994; the intention is to analyse the meteorological and surface conditions using special balloons.

Below: *A Viking image of Valles Marineris, the canyon formed by faulting, erosion and landslides which may be up to 8km (5 miles) deep.*

The Minor Planets

Mainly found between the orbits of Mars and Jupiter are the minor planets, also known as the asteroids, which are thought to be material left over from when the Solar System was formed and which never collected together to form a planet. The asteroids are quite small; the largest of them is Ceres which is only around 1,000km (620 miles) in diameter.

Around 3,500 asteroids have now had their orbits calculated, and astronomers believe that there may be as many as a million of these tiny objects orbiting the Sun. However, in spite of these large numbers, if all the asteroids were collected together they would form a world smaller than the Moon.

Although most asteroids keep to the area between Mars and Jupiter, there are seveal groups which travel away from this region. These include the Trojans, two groups of asteroids which travel around the Sun along Jupiter's orbit; Amor asteroids which cross the orbit of Mars; and Apollo asteroids which cross the Earth's orbit. Some asteroids, known as Earth-grazers, make very close approaches to our planet, the closest approach in modern times being that of an object designated 1989FC which missed us by a mere 700,000km (435,000 miles) on the night of 22/23 March 1989. Had an impact occurred, a great deal of damage would have been caused.

JUPITER AND SATURN

Jupiter

Jupiter is the largest planetary member of the Sun's family with a diameter of some 12 times that of the Earth. A gas planet, Jupiter is thought to contain a solid rocky core above which is a deep atmosphere comprised mainly of hydrogen and helium gases.

Jupiter has the shortest axial rotation period or "day" of any planet in the Solar System. This has produced a marked polar flattening which is the result of outward-acting centrifugal forces set up by Jupiter's rapid axial spin which have pushed out Jupiter's equatorial regions.

The atmosphere is subject to constant activity and by far the most famous feature is the Great Red Spot, a huge oval formation located in Jupiter's southern hemisphere. First seen by the Italian astronomer Giovanni Cassini in 1665, it is thought to be a colossal atmospheric storm. It is certainly impressive; observation has shown that it varies in size and can reach a length of around 40,000km (25,000 miles)!

The Jovian Ring System and Satellites

Jupiter has a ring system discovered by Voyager 1 in 1979. The inner ring is faint and has a width of some 20,000km (12,400 miles). The main ring section is 6,400km (4,000 miles) wide and 30km (19 miles) thick, and is in turn surrounded by the still fainter outer ring which reaches out to a distance of around 100,000km (62,000 miles).

There are 16 satellites in all. The four largest of these — Io, Europa, Ganymede and Callisto — were discovered in 1610

Right: *A Voyager 1 image of Jupiter's colourful outer atmosphere and cloud layers taken from 32.7 million km (20 million miles) away. Note the vivid belts and zones: the bright zones are those with rising gas; the darker belts are cooler regions of descending material.*

by the Italian astronomer Galileo Galilei and are known collectively as the Galilean satellites. The German astronomer Simon Marius is also credited with their discovery, made quite independently of that of Galileo. The other Jovian moons are all quite small in comparison to the Galilean satellites.

Saturn

Like Jupiter, Saturn has a marked polar flattening and it also has belts and zones, although less impressive than Jupiter's. It does, however, have a glorious ring system. Visible even through a small telescope, the rings are made up of tiny icy particles around Saturn's equatorial plane.

When seen through Earth-based telescopes, the rings are divided into three main sections. The brightest B-ring lies inside the somewhat fainter A-ring. The faintest C-ring, or Crepe Ring, is the innermost of the three.

In 1979 the American space probe Pioneer 11 flew past Saturn and discovered a faint ring outside the A-ring. This was named the F-ring and its discovery was quickly followed by that of the D-ring, found inside the Crepe Ring. The D-ring was discovered by the Voyager 1 and 2 spacecraft in 1980 and 1981, their cameras also bringing to light the E- and G-rings which are two very faint rings situated well beyond the main ring system.

Below: *Saturn with three of its moons; from the left: Rhea, Dione and Tethys whose shadow falls on the southern hemisphere.*

Above: *The different chemical composition in Saturn's rings are indicated by colour variations in this picture taken by Voyager.*

Saturn's Satellites

Saturn has a total of 18 satellites, the largest of which is Titan. This 5,150km (3,200 mile) diameter world was discovered by the Dutch astronomer Christiaan Huygens in 1655.

When the Voyager 1 space probe passed Titan in 1980, it revealed a world completely enveloped in a thick atmosphere hiding its surface from view. The temperature on Titan is thought to be around −180°C, close to the triple point of methane. This means that methane may exist in solid, liquid or gaseous form, just as water does here on Earth.

There are another four satellites with substantial diameters, these being Tethys, Dione, Rhea and Iapetus. The other satellites are smaller, irregularly-shaped objects.

URANUS AND NEPTUNE

Uranus

Uranus was discovered in 1781 by William Herschel, although its great distance from the Sun meant that little was known about the planet until the flyby of Voyager 2 in January 1986. The Voyager cameras revealed a banded atmosphere which was somewhat less impressive than those of Jupiter and Saturn. Methane clouds were spotted above the Uranian southern hemisphere, the temperature in their vicinity being around −210°C.

Uranus has a ring system. It was first discovered on 10 March 1977 as Uranus passed in front of, or occulted, a faint star. As this occurred the star's light was seen to disappear temporarily, as expected. Yet it also disappeared several times both before and after, leading astronomers to the conclusion that a system of rings existed around Uranus, the rings producing a series of shorter occultations. The Voyager 2 cameras increased the number of known rings from nine to 11.

Ten new satellites were also discovered, bringing the known total to 15. Most of the newly-discovered moons were tracked only long enough to have their orbits, diameters and distances from Uranus calculated, although Voyager 2 revealed much information about the five previously-known moons. Of particular interest was Miranda, which provided the most surprises for the Voyager scientists. This small world contains

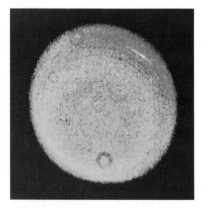

Left: *A false-colour image of Uranus. It orbits the Sun on its side and the south pole (near the centre here) will be in darkness until 2007.*

Right: *Neptune's Great and Small Dark Spots (centre left and lower right). It is blue due to the methane absorbing the red light.*

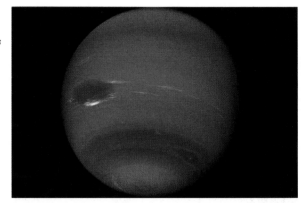

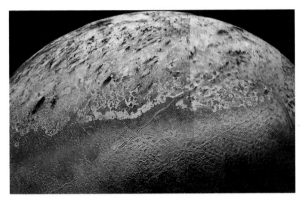

Above: *The reflectivity of Triton's south polar cap (bottom half of picture) suggests a covering with a nitrogen ice layer.*

examples of practically every type of geological feature known to us here on Earth, including craters, valleys and canyons, grooved terrain, huge mountains, faults, cliffs and several large plateaux!

Neptune

Uranus was seen to be wandering from its predicted orbit and astronomers thought that this was due to the gravitational influence of another, undiscovered planet. Two mathematicians, the Englishman John Couch Adams and the Frenchman Urbain Jean Joseph Leverrier, calculated the position of the hypothetical planet. Both Adams and Leverrier used similar methods to calculate where the planet should be, although neither knew that the other was working on the same problem.

The planet eventually came to light in 1846 when astronomers at the Berlin Observatory carried out a search using Leverrier's calculations. Because the results of both Adams and Leverrier were in close agreement, the mathematicians have been given equal credit for their work.

Neptune, as the new planet was named, after the Roman God of the Sea, became the most distant world to be visited by a spacecraft when Voyager 2 passed the planet in August 1989. Among the discoveries made by Voyager was a system of three narrow rings girdling the planet. The Neptunian atmosphere was found to be more active than that of Uranus, with several individual features being seen.

The atmosphere contains belts and zones, the most impressive of these being in the southern hemisphere. A number of cloud features were seen, the most prominent being the Great Dark Spot. This feature, together with the similar but less impressive Small Dark Spot, was located south of the Neptunian equator. Wind speeds on Neptune vary with altitude and both features travel around the planet at different rates. The Small Dark Spot takes 16 hours to complete one revoltuon, over two hours less than the Great Dark Spot.

The number of known Neptunian satellites was increased from two to eight. The largest moon, Triton, was found to play host to a number of interesting geological features including fault lines crossing its surface and a bright polar region. There is a lack of craters, something which has been put down to volcanic activity over the past few hundred million years which may have covered up any impact craters there may have been.

PLUTO AND CHARON

Named after the mythological Greek Guardian of the Underworld, Pluto is the outermost planetary member of the Solar System. Pluto's orbit is highly eccentric and its distance from the Sun varies greatly. For a 20-year period during each of its 248-year long journeys around the Sun, Pluto crosses the orbital path of Neptune. This last happened in 1979 and until 1999 Nepture will remain the outermost planet.

The existence of Pluto was suspected long before its eventual discovery in 1930. Neptune was seen to be straying from its predicted orbit and astronomers believed that the observed discrepancies in Neptune's orbital motion were due to the gravitational influence of another, as yet undiscovered, planet.

Several astronomers carried out an unsuccessful search for the proposed planet. Notable among those who tried was

Right: *These images are sections from the two plates which led to the discovery of Pluto. Clyde Tombaugh's extensive search for Lowell's trans-Neptunian planet finally paid off in January 1930. On the 23rd of that month (left) he took a picture of stars in the constellation of Gemini, followed by another on the 29th (right) showing that an object had moved against the stars.*

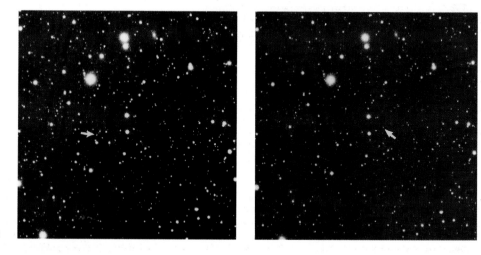

the American Percival Lowell and, although he was unsuccessful in his efforts, his work was to contribute directly to the eventual discovery.

Prior to his death in 1916, Lowell gave instructions for the construction of a special wide-field camera which was to be used in the search. The camera was designed to take photographs of different areas of the sky, each area being photographed twice with exposures taken a few days apart. An image of any object that moved across the sky during this interval would appear in different positions on the plates, unlike those of stars whose positions would match.

In 1929 the camera was ready and a young astronomer named Clyde Tombaugh set out to try and locate the proposed planet. He took a huge number of photographs and, during his search, examined countless images. Eventually he discovered a starlike point of light which had moved between two exposures and which could not be accounted for by any known object. At last, the new planet had been found.

Because of Pluto's immense distance, little was known about the planet until quite recently. The first major breakthrough in our knowledge of Pluto came in 1978 when the American astronomer James W. Christy spotted a peculiar "bump" on the edge of a photograph of Pluto. Further examination revealed similar bumps on previously-taken pictures and Christy came to the conclusion that these were actually images of a satellite orbiting Pluto.

In keeping with tradition the new satellite was named Charon after the boatman who, according to legend, ferried dead souls across the River Styx to Pluto's underworld domain. Both Pluto and Charon are thought to be comprised of a mixture of methane ice and rock. The diameter of Charon

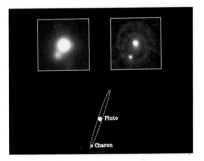

Right: *The best Earth-based picture of Pluto and Charon (upper left) and an image taken by the Hubble Space Telescope (upper right). The diagram shows the relative positions of Pluto and Charon at the time.*

is 1,280km (795 miles), roughly half the diameter of Pluto itself, and it completes one orbit of Pluto every six days, nine hours and 57 minutes at a mean distance of 18,265km (11,350 miles). Charon's orbital period matches exactly the axial rotation period of Pluto which means that Pluto and Charon are gravitationally locked to each other. To an observer on Pluto, Charon would remain permanently suspended in the same position in the sky.

Is Pluto an escaped satellite of Neptune? Did Pluto come into being as a result of the processes by which the other planetary members of the Solar System were formed? The answers to these questions remain unanswered and the origins of this tiny planet and its satellite are, as yet, unknown. There is speculation that Pluto may be one of a swarm of small objects orbiting the Sun in this region. If this is the case, further discoveries from what could be called a secondary asteroid belt could be made in the future. Whatever the origin and true identity of Pluto, only time will tell.

COMETS

Although they can appear impressive, comets are in reality only minor members of the Solar System. They are comprised of a frozen mixture of dust and gas and have little mass. They are believed to originate from a vast cloud of primaeval matter located in the outer regions of the Solar System. The existence of this cloud was first suggested by the Dutch astronomer Jan Oort in 1950 and is known as Oort's Cloud in his honour.

Within Oort's Cloud comets exist in the form of icy chunks, taking on their characteristic appearance only after leaving the cloud and travelling towards the inner regions of the Solar System. Once a comet nears the Sun, the energy from our star acts upon it. The comet is heated, causing the ice to vaporise and release dust and gas. This material then forms a head, or "coma", around the original comet, which in turn becomes the nucleus. Solar energy continues to act upon the comet, eventually forcing dust and gas away from the nucleus to form one or more tails. These tails are comprised of either gas (ion tails) or dust.

As a comet rounds the Sun and heads off once more towards the outer Solar System, the effects of solar energy decrease. The tails and coma disappear, leaving the icy nucleus to continue its orbit. The comet may return to the cloud, or it may be pulled into a shorter orbit by the gravitational influence of one of the major planets.

The shortest known orbital period for a comet is that of 3.3 years for Encke's Comet. Halley's Comet, on the other hand, takes 76 years to travel once around the Sun. Some comets

Above: *Comet IRAS-Araki-Alcock was first seen in 1983 in images produced by the technology of the Infra Red Astronomy Satellite.*

have much longer periods, many of which are so long that astronomers are unable to predict their return with accuracy.

Normally, comets are named after their discoverers. Halley's Comet, for example, was named after Edmund Halley, the astronomer who realised that bright comets seen in 1531, 1607 and 1682 were actually the same object. Halley calculated that it would reappear in 1759. He was correct and the comet was duly named in his honour as the astronomer who had predicted its return.

Until quite recently, all our observation of comets was carried out through Earth-based telescopes. The return of

Right: *Colour-coded image taken on 8 March 1976 of Comet West, one of the most impressive for years.*

Left: *Twilight forms the backdrop for this picture of Halley's Comet which was taken in Chile in 1986.*

Halley's Comet in 1985/86, however, was to see a huge advance in our methods of cometary observation. Several space probes, including the Japanese Sakigake and Suisei craft and the two Soviet Vega probes, were sent to intercept Halley's Comet and make observations from close range.

However, the most successful of the probes to Halley's Comet was the European Giotto which passed within 610km (380 miles) of the nucleus on 14 March 1986. Before being put out of action by debris from the comet, Giotto's cameras revealed an irregularly-shaped nucleus measuring around 15km x 8km (9 miles x 5 miles). Material was seen emerging from vents in the surface of the nucleus which went to form the cometary coma and tails.

When comets pass through the solar neighbourhood they lose material into space. As we shall see, there is a link between this material and the appearance in our skies of meteors, or shooting stars.

METEORS AND METEORITES

Interplanetary space is littered with debris ranging in size from large chunks, with diameters up to several kilometres, down to tiny particles of dust. These objects are called meteoroids and all are travelling around the Sun in their own orbits, rather like tiny planets.

While in space, meteoroids are too small and faint to be seen, although they may occasionally wander close to our planet. If this happens, the meteoroid may succumb to the Earth's gravitational pull. They then enter the atmosphere at incredibly high speeds, colliding with air particles as they do so. The friction causes the meteoroid to burn up, producing a streak of light in the sky that we call a meteor or "shooting star". Very bright meteors are called fireballs.

Meteor Showers

There are two types of meteor: *sporadic* meteors can enter the atmosphere at any time and from any direction; *shower* meteors, on the other hand, are associated with comets. As we have seen, comets shed particles as they pass through the inner solar system, these particles becoming spread out all along the orbital path of the comet. The Earth crosses numerous cometary orbits during its journey around the Sun and when this happens there is an increase in the number of particles entering the atmosphere. We refer to these increases in meteor activity as meteor showers.

The particles emanating from comets move around the Sun, and so enter the atmosphere, in parallel paths. The meteors we see in any particular shower, therefore, all appear to radiate

Above: *A bright, bursting meteor captured on film on 16 March 1975 just below the star Rigel in the constellation of Orion.*

from the same point in the sky. This point is called the radiant. A similar effect is seen when we look along a long, straight railway. Although the rails are parallel, they appear to converge in the distance. The point at which the rails appear to meet is analogous to a meteor shower radiant.

There are over 20 annual meteor showers, some of which produce lots of meteors. These showers are named after the area of sky containing the radiant. For example, the radiant of the Ophiuchids lies in the constellation Ophiuchus, while the Perseids (the most active shower of all) appear to radiate from a point in the constellation Perseus. The Perseids are associated with Comet Swift-Tuttle and are seen during July/August. Providing the sky is dark, clear and moonless, as many as 70 meteors or more per hour may be observed.

Below: *The huge meteorite impact crater in Arizona, USA, is nearly 200 metres deep and has a rim rising some 50 metres high.*

Right: *About 95 per cent of meteorite falls are classified as stony. One of the best examples of the "aerolite" type, as they are also known, is from Paragould, Arkansas, USA, and weighs 335kg (745lb).*

Meteorites

Any particle that is large enough to survive its passage through the atmosphere and hit the surface of our planet is called a meteorite. Meteorite falls are quite rare, although many museums have collections of these objects. The largest known meteorite is a 60 tonne object lying where it fell at Hoba West in South West Africa. Most are stone meteorites, but two other classes exist: so-called iron ones and an in-between variety called "tektites" which consist of glass similar to obsidian.

Prior to the early 19th century, the origin of meteorites was something of a mystery. However, in 1803 the French physicist Jean Baptiste Biot showed that meteorites were extraterrestrial in origin. Many meteorites are thought to originate within the Asteroid Belt from collisions between larger objects.

The surfaces of the Earth and Moon, together with those of other planets and satellites, bear the scars of meteorite impacts in the form of craters. One of the most impressive here on Earth is near Canon Diablo in Arizona, U.S.A. Over a kilometre in diameter, this feature was formed following an impact which took place thousands of years ago.

AURORAE

The Earth is surrounded by a huge magnetic field produced by movements within the liquid outer core of our planet. These movements generate a dynamo effect which produce electrical currents. These are pushed outwards by the rotation of our planet to create a magnetic field, or magnetosphere, which extends to many thousands of kilometres out into space.

The energized particles coming from the Sun (the solar wind) meet the magnetosphere at the magnetopause and are generally deflected around the Earth by the magnetosheath, a region which envelops the magnetosphere. Yet not all particles are deflected. A number find their way through the magnetopause and enter the Van Allen radiation belts. These large, doughnut-shaped regions contain charged solar particles which are in constant motion between the Earth's magnetic poles.

There are two Van Allen belts, an inner and an outer, and normally they manage to hold on to their quota of charged particles, but they can become overloaded. This happens when the number of particles leaving the Sun increases, either as a result of increased sunspot activity or following the appearance of large solar flares. At these times the Van Allen belts become overloaded and energized particles spill out into the upper atmosphere.

These particles collide with air particles producing reactions which cause atoms of oxygen and nitrogen in the atmosphere to glow. We see these glows as auroral displays and they are generally visible from locations near the Earth's magnetic poles. Displays which take place in the northern hemisphere are known as the aurora borealis, those seen in the south being referred to as aurora australis. They occur at heights of anything between 100 and 1,000kms (60 and 620miles) and can take on any number of widely different visual forms.

Right: *A beautiful, greenish auroral display photographed from Cumbria in the n th-west of England during October 1981.*

Right: *Aurorae can last for hours on end and may display a number of colours, but mainly they are red, green and blue. This red glow on 12 April 1981 provides a majestic backdrop for a dome of the Kitt Peak National Observatory. Other, less spectacular phenomena exist too: Zodiacal Light is a faint reflective glow seen pre-dawn or after dusk; while Gegenschein is a faint Solar counter-glow in the sky.*

Although aurorae can be fairly stable and docile, they can vary in appearance over short periods. An unspectacular glow on the horizon may expand to form huge arcs or bands of light crossing the sky. Patches of auroral light, resembling ghostly clouds, may also cross the sky. The lines of magnetic force running between the Earth's magnetic poles may pull the particles which form the aurora into huge rays which stretch out from the arcs and bands. The appearance of these rays has been likened to huge cosmic searchlights reaching up into the night sky.

Really vivid auroral displays are not common and once seen are not forgotten. It is well worth keeping an eye on your northern horizon (or southern horizon if you live in the southern hemisphere) for any aurorae that may appear, particularly during periods of increased solar activity, for they are a memorable experience.

STELLAR EVOLUTION

A Star is Born
Stars are formed inside huge interstellar clouds of gas and dust called nebulae, and develop through extremely long periods of time into white dwarfs, neutron stars or black holes. Stars are born following a process known as gravitational collapse whereby clumps of material form inside the nebula. As the clumps grow, their internal temperature and pressure increase until a point is reached when nuclear reactions, similar to those taking place within the Sun, are triggered off. The thermal energy generated acts outwards, halting the inward collapse through gravity. These hot, dense and relatively stable regions in the nebula are called protostars.

Beginning to Shine
What happens next depends on the mass of the protostar. If it is similar to that of our Sun, nuclear fusion will occur at the core where the temperature is in the region of 15 million °C (28 million °F). During the process, four hydrogen atoms are crushed together to form one atom of helium. A tiny amount of mass is left over from the reaction which makes its way to the surface from where it escapes into space as light and heat and the star begins to shine.

The star continues to shine, fuelled by its supply of hydrogen. A star with a mass similar to that of the Sun will shine for around 10,000 million years. Stars with lower mass may shine longer, their hydrogen being used up at a slower rate. Conversely, bigger stars use their hydrogen up quicker. Eventually, whatever the star's mass, the ratio of hydrogen

Above: *Traces of the nebula from which these stars formed can still be seen around the open star cluster of the Pleiades.*

to helium changes and the star enters yet another stage of its evolution.

Red Giants and White Dwarfs
When the heat emitted by the star is reduced, there will be a corresponding reduction in the outward-acting thermal energy and the star will have difficulty supporting its outer

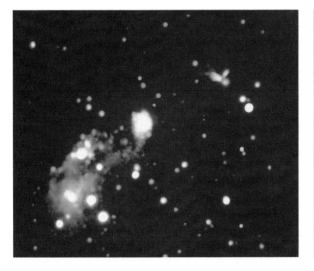

Above: *An infrared image of NGC 7538, a region of massive star formation lying at a distance of around 7,000 light years.*

Above: *A naked eye view of the red giant star Antares, captured at the upper right of this picture of Sagittarius and Scorpius.*

layers. Gravity will begin to take over and the core will become compressed, eventually being reduced to a fraction of its original size but with a greatly-increased temperature and density. There is a further increase in outward-acting thermal energy which forces the star's outer layers to expand into surrounding space. The star becomes a "red giant" with a surface temperature in the region of 3,500°C (6,300°F).

There are many such red giants in the sky and our Sun will joint their ranks in around 5,000 million years, increasing its luminosity by around a hundred times as it does so.

The core continues to compress, eventually triggering off further reactions whereby the helium is turned into carbon. Once the helium fuel runs out, two different things can occur: low mass stars (anything less than 1.4 times the mass of the Sun) will cease further nuclear reactions and the star will cool down and collapse to form a white dwarf whose heat will eventually radiate into space, leaving a dead star called a black dwarf; higher mass stars form neutron stars.

Supernovae and Neutron Stars

Stars with masses of between 1.4 and 3 times that of the Sun undergo such gravitational contraction that their constituent protons and electrons are crushed together to form neutrons. The resultant neutron stars are so dense that a single table-spoonful of neutron star material would weigh around 15 million tonnes!

Below: *NGC 3132 is a planetary nebula in Vela — gases blown out from the core of a star about to collapse into a white dwarf.*

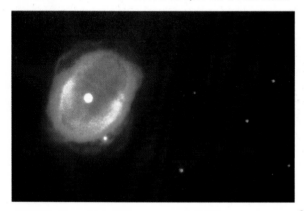

Above: *A colour-enhanced image of the Crab Nebula M1 (NGC 1952) in Taurus. It is the remnant of a supernova observed exploding in 1054AD and is the brightest example known.*

Above: *Supernova S1987A is visible to the right of the centre in this view of a portion of the Large Magellanic Cloud.*

The existence of neutron stars, although suspected, was not proved until 1967 when bursts of radio emission were detected from an invisible source in space. The signals received were being transmitted at a very precise and regular rate and astronomers believed that they were coming from a star that was pulsating, leading to it being christened a "pulsar".

The process of collapse of such massive stars is much more violent than that by which planetary nebulae are formed. The collapse causes a sudden increase in the star's internal temperature, producing a violent nuclear reaction which hurls the outer layers into surrounding space. This event is called a supernova and it can, for a short time, outshine the entire galaxy of which it is a member!

Following the explosion, the core of the star collapses to form a neutron star. These spin rapidly and emit radio pulses synchronous with their rotation. Since 1967 many more pulsars have been found, although only a few have been identified optically.

Black Holes
Stars with eight-plus solar masses may suffer a totally irresistible gravitational contraction. As the size decreases and the density grows, the star's escape velocity increases until it exceeds the speed of light. At this point, the object would become invisible to a nearby observer. As distance from the collapsed star increases, the gravitational pull lessens until a point is reached from which light can escape. This is the event horizon. Just beneath this is a spherical volume of space forever hidden from view. This region is a black hole and marks the final stage in the evolution of very massive stars.

Although we cannot actually see a black hole the evidence for their existence has come about from the study of binary star systems. Astronomers can, by carefully observing their behaviour and orbital motion, calculate the masses of the stars forming a binary system. Binaries are often found to contain one massive component and a few have been found to play host to stars which are simply too massive to be either a white dwarf or neutron star. An example is the X-ray system Cygnus X-1, the optical component of which is the supergiant star HDE 226868. The invisible component of the Cygnus X-1 system has a very high mass and is thought by many astronomers to be a black hole.

THE STARS

When we look up on a dark, clear night the sky seems to be filled with millions of stars, but in reality only a couple of thousand or so are visible at any one time. The stars are grouped into patterns, or constellations, although the stars within any particular group are not necessarily associated with each other. The stars all lie at different distances and their apparent closeness to each other is usually nothing more than a line of sight effect.

There is a total of 88 constellations, many of which depict characters from mythology. The stars close to the South Celestial Pole, however, were only discovered during the recent past and as a result many groups in this area of sky have modern-sounding names, such as Telescopium (The Telescope) and Horologium (The Pendulum Clock).

The Celestial Sphere

Our conception of the sky is that of an imaginary sphere completely surrounding the Earth. We call this the celestial sphere, the stars themselves appearing as points of light fixed to its inner surface. Objects that move through the sky, such as the Sun, Moon and planets, appear to travel against the backdrop of stars.

As the Earth spins on its axis the celestial sphere appears to rotate, with the west to east rotation of the Earth producing an apparent east to west rotation of the celestial sphere. You get the same effect by standing in the middle of a room and spinning round; as you spin the walls of the room appear to rotate in the opposite direction.

The result of the Earth's spin is that the stars and other celestial objects appear to rise in the east, cross the sky and set in the west. The Earth's rotation also gives rise to day and night; it is daytime on the hemisphere facing the Sun and nightime on the opposite one.

The Earth rotates around an imaginary line passing between the North and South Poles. This line is called the axis of rotation. If we extend this axis up into the sky it will "meet" the celestial sphere at two points. We call these points the North and South Celestial Poles (see pages 40-41 and 60-63).

Below: *A stationary camera centred on Polaris with the lens open for some hours captured these star trails around the North Pole.*

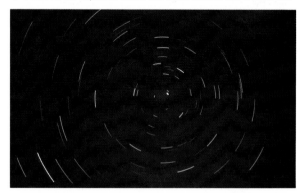

As the Earth rotates so the stars appear to move around the celestial poles.

Another important feature of the celestial sphere is the celestial equator. This is a line around the celestial sphere lying directly above the Earth's equator. Stars that lie to the north of the celestial equator are known as northern hemisphere stars, while those to the south are referred to as southern hemisphere stars.

The 88 Constellations

Latin name	English version	Latin name	English version	Latin name	English version
Andromeda	Andromeda	Crux	Cross	Orion	Orion
Antlia	Air Pump	Cygnus	Swan	Pavo	Peacock
Apus	Bird of Paradise	Delphinus	Dolphin	Pegasus	Pegasus
Aquarius	Water Carrier	Dorado	Goldfish	Perseus	Perseus
Aquila	Eagle	Draco	Dragon	Phoenix	Phoenix
Ara	Altar	Equuleus	Foal	Pictor	Painter's Easel
Aries	Ram	Eridanus	River Eridanus	Pisces	Fishes
Auriga	Charioteer	Fornax	Furnace	Piscis Austrinus	Southern Fish
Boötes	Herdsman	Gemini	Twins	Puppis	Poop
Caelum	Graving Tool	Grus	Crane	Pyxis	Mariner's Compass
Camelopardalis	Giraffe	Hercules	Hercules	Reticulum	Net
Cancer	Crab	Horologium	Pendulum Clock	Sagitta	Arrow
Canes Venatici	Hunting Dogs	Hydra	Water Snake	Sagittarius	Archer
Canis Major	Great Dog	Hydrus	Little Water Snake	Scorpius	Scorpion
Canis Minor	Little Dog	Indus	Indian	Sculptor	Sculptor
Capricornus	Goat (or Sea-Goat)	Lacerta	Lizard	Scutum	Shield
Carina	Keel	Leo	Lion	Serpens	Serpent
Cassiopeia	Cassiopeia	Leo Minor	Little Lion	Sextans	Sextant
Centaurus	Centaur	Lepus	Hare	Taurus	Bull
Cepheus	Cepheus	Libra	Scales	Telescopium	Telescope
Cetus	Whale	Lupus	Wolf	Triangulum	Triangle
Chameleon	Chameleon	Lynx	Lynx	Triangulum Australe	Southern Triangle
Circinus	Compasses	Lyra	Lyre	Tucana	Toucan
Columba	Dove	Mensa	Table Mountain	Ursa Major	Great Bear
Coma Berenices	Berenice's Hair	Microscopium	Microscope	Ursa Minor	Little Bear
Corona Australis	Southern Crown	Monoceros	Unicorn	Vela	Sails
Corona Borealis	Northern Crown	Musca	Fly	Virgo	Virgin
Corvus	Crow	Norma	Level	Volans	Flying Fish
Crater	Cup	Octans	Octant	Vulpecula	Fox
		Ophiuchus	Serpent Bearer		

Distances to the Stars

The stars and other objects beyond the Solar System are so far away from us that it is useless to try and express their distances in miles or kilometres. Instead, atronomers use a much larger unit of distance called a light year. A light year is the distance a ray of light would travel in a year. At the speed of 300,000km (186,000 miles) per second this is equal to 9,460,000,000,000km (5,910,000,000,000 miles).

The Nearest Stars

Star	Constellation	Apparent Magnitude	Distance (Light Years)
Proxima Centauri	Centaurus	+10.7	4.3
Alpha Centauri*	Centaurus	− 0.27	4.34
Barnard's Star	Ophiuchus	+ 9.5	6.0
Wolf 359	Leo	+13.6	7.7
Lalande 21185	Ursa Major	+ 7.6	8.3
Sirius*	Canis Major	− 1.42	8.7
Luyten 726-8*	Cetus	+12.3	9.0
Ross 154	Sagittarius	+10.6	9.5
Ross 248	Andromeda	+12.2	10.3
Epsilon Eridani	Eridanus	+ 3.7	10.8
Luyten 789-6	Aquarius	+12.2	10.8
Ross 128	Virgo	+11.1	10.9
61 Cygni*	Cygnus	+ 5.2	11.1
Procyon*	Canis Minor	+ 0.35	11.3
Epsilon Indi	Indus	+ 4.7	11.4
Sigma 2398*	Draco	+ 8.8	11.4
Groombridge 34*	Andromeda	+ 8.0	11.7
Tau Ceti	Cetus	+ 3.5	11.8
Lacaille 9352	Piscis Austrinus	+ 7.4	11.9
BD +5°1668	Canis Minor	+ 9.8	12.3

*denotes that the star has a companion

Stellar Magnitudes

In around 150BC the Greek astronomer Hipparchus devised a system to express the apparent brightness, or magnitudes, of stars. He rated the brightest stars as 1st class and the faintest as 6th. Although refined somewhat, the same basic system is used today and modern instruments allow astronomers to grade stellar brightness to within 0.01 of a magnitude. Very bright objects, such as the Sun (−26.8) and Alpha Centauri (−0.27), have negative magnitude values. The faintest naked eye objects are around 6th magnitude, while the faintest ones visible through large telescopes have magnitudes of around 28.

A 1st magnitude star is 100 times as bright as one of 6th magnitude. In other words, stars of successive magnitudes differ in brightness by a factor of 2.512. This means that a star of magnitude 2.00 is 2.512 times as bright as one of magnitude 3.00 and 6.31 times (2.512 x 2.512) as bright as one of magnitude 4.00 and so on.

This sytem describes the *apparent* magnitude of a star and gives no real indication of its true luminosity. For example, the star Sirius has an apparent magnitude of −1.42, brighter than Canopus at apparent magnitude −0.72. Yet Canopus is actually much more luminous than Sirius, only appearing fainter because it lies so much further away.

Angular Measurement

Distances between points on the celestial sphere are expressed in angles. For example, the two stars Merak and Dubhe in The Plough (see page 41) or big dipper are 5° apart. This means that an angle of 5° would be formed at the eye by two lines, one extended to Merak and the other to Dubhe.

Smaller angles, such as the distances between the components of a double star or the diameter of an object such as the Sun, Moon or a planet, are expressed in minutes and seconds. One degree is divided into 60 minutes (60′) and each minute is further divided into 60 seconds (60″). For example, the angular diameter of the full Moon is 30′; in other words, the angle formed at the eye by lines of sight to either side of the lunar disc is 30′, or half a degree. Most measurements amount to no more than a few seconds.

Right: *The human hand can provide a useful indicator of distances between points on the celestial sphere. When held at arms length the clenched fist spans roughly 10° of the sky — equal to the distance between the top two stars in the "bowl" of The Plough or Big Dipper. The outstretched hand spans some 20°, a finger equal to 1°. The Plough itself is some 25° in length, less than the 30° from Dubhe to the Pole Star (page 41).*

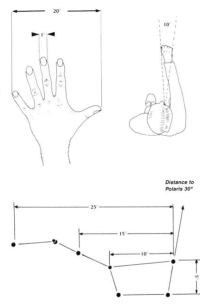

Distance to Polaris 30°

The Brightest Stars			
Star	Constellation	Apparent Magnitude	Distance (Light Years)
Sirius	Canis Major	−1.42	8.7
Canopus	Carina	−0.72	1170
Alpha Centauri	Centaurus	−0.27	4.34
Arcturus	Bootes	−0.06	37
Vega	Lyra	+0.04	27
Capella	Auriga	0.06	45
Rigel	Orion	0.14	900
Procyon	Canis Minor	0.35	11.3
Achernar	Eridanus	0.53	120
Hadar	Centaurus	0.66	490
Betelgeuse	Orion	0.70 (v)	520
Altair	Aquila	0.77	16
Aldebaran	Taurus	0.86	68
Acrux	Crux	0.87	370
Antares	Scorpius	0.92 (v)	520
Spica	Virgo	1.00 (v)	275
Pollux	Gemini	1.16	35
Fomalhaut	Piscis Austrinus	1.17	23
Deneb	Cygnus	1.26	1600
Beta Crucis	Crux	1.28	490

(v) denotes that the star is variable

Star Names

Around 200 stars have proper names of Greek, Roman or Arabic origin, although only a few of these are in common use. Examples are Betelgeuse in Orion and Castor in Gemini. Many stars are assigned Greek letters, a system devised by the German astronomer Johann Bayer in 1603 and used for the brighter members of a constellation. The brightest star in a particular group is called Alpha, the second brightest Beta and so on. The Greek letter is followed by the genitive case of the constellation name. (This is simply the Latin form meaning ''of'' the constellation.)

Most of the brightest stars have both proper names and Greek letters, an example being Acrux in Crux which is also known as Alpha Crucis. (There are confusing instances where the Greek lettering system is not rigidly adhered to in terms of descending brightness: Castor is also known as as Alpha Geminorum in spite of the fact that Castor is the second brightest star in the group. The brightest member of Gemini is acutally Pollux, which is also designated Beta Geminorum.)

Using the Star Charts

The charts on the following pages show the main stars and constellations visible throughout the year. There are two charts which show the stars close to the North and South Celestial Poles. The stars around the North Celestial Pole are observable only from the northern hemisphere, and then only from mid-latitudes and northwards. Those around the South Celestial Pole are observable from corresponding latitudes in the southern hemisphere.

The main charts show the stars between these two regions, key stars and constellations linking the various charts. The best times of year to view each region of sky are given in the text accompanying the charts. Compass points are given, where needed, and they should be aligned accordingly prior to observation. (Note that with celestial directions the east and west points are reversed, with east to the left).

The charts show the sky as seen by northern hemisphere observers when looking at the region of sky lying roughly between the overhead point and the southern horizon. For those below the equator the area of sky covered lies roughly between the overhead point and the northern horizon. Those fortunate enough to live at or near the equator will be able to observe all the stars depicted at one time or another.

The reason that most of us cannot view all the stars shown is simply because the Earth gets in the way! Imagine being an observer in London, or a location at a similar latitude, and using the chart showing the stars around Orion and Eridanus (see page 43). Although the constellations Lepus and Fornax will be visible low over the southern horizon, those further to the south, such as Caelum and Horologium, will be below the southern horizon, hidden from view by the bulk of our planet. In order to see these groups, our observer would have to travel south. As he did so, more and more stars would come into view as he moved further and further around the planet. A similar effect is seen by someone watching a ship approaching over the horizon. When below the horizon the ship is hidden by the curve of our planet and only becomes more visible as it gets closer to the observer.

Right: *The prominent cruciform-shaped Crux together with, at lower left, The Coalsack, a huge patch of dust which absorbs starlight and obscures part of the Milky Way which it straddles.*

The Catalogues of Messier and Dreyer

During the latter part of the eighteenth century, the French astronomer Charles Messier spent much of his time searching for new comets. At the time of discovery, a comet is generally a long way from the Sun and appears as nothing more than a fuzzy patch of light. During his searches Messier stumbled across a number of objects that had comet-like appearances; unlike comets, however, which would move through the sky over a period of time and therefore give their presence away, the objects Messier saw remained stationary. In order to avoid confusion, Messier drew up a catalogue of the objects he confused with comets. It is ironic that although Messier discovered many comets he is best remembered today for his catalogue of non-cometary objects!

As well as showing the main stars and constellations the charts show numerous other objects too which are of great interest and which may require a telescope. These include star clusters, nebulae and galaxies. Some of these have proper names, such as the Orion Nebula (see page 47) or the Sombrero Hat Galaxy (see page 49), but many are designated either by M numbers (eg M42) or NGC numbers (eg NGC2168). The M number refers to the entry for that object in Messier's Catalogue; an NGC number refers to the reference for the object in the *New General Catalogue of Nebulae and Clusters of Stars* drawn up by the astronomer J. L. E. Dreyer in 1888. Dreyer's catalogue contains several thousand objects, while that of Messier contains only 110. Messier himself only included 103 objects in his original catalogue, a further seven having been added in more recent times. Dreyer's catalogue also has two supplements, the *Index Catalogues*, and these objects carry IC numbers.

THE NORTH CIRCUMPOLAR STARS

The Earth's axis is aligned with two points in the sky; known as the North and South Celestial Poles they appear directly overhead in the sky when viewed from the terrestrial poles. As the Earth spins on its axis, the stars appear to revolve around the celestial poles. The position of the North Celestial Pole is marked almost exactly by the 2nd magnitude star Polaris, also known as The Pole Star, the leading star of Ursa Minor (The Little Bear). Observers in the southern hemisphere are not so lucky; their "pole star" is the dim, 5th magnitude star Sigma Octantis which lies in the obscure constellation Octans (The Octant) (see page 61).

This area of sky contains a number of famous constellations including Ursa Major (The Great Bear). Although comprised mainly of faint stars its seven brightest members form The Plough, or, as it is called in the United States, Big Dipper, a conspicuous group which is probably the best-known pattern of stars in the entire sky.

Double Stars

Most stars are not alone in space, but belong to groups comprising of two or more members. As well as double stars there are triple, quadruple and multiple stars as well as the much larger star clusters.

There are two basic types of double star. Optical doubles are formed from two stars which lie in more or less the same line of sight as seen from Earth. In reality one star may be much further away from us, their apparent closeness to each other being no more than a line of sight effect. Binary stars are formed from stars which are gravitationally linked and which orbit around their common centre of gravity.

There are many double stars visible to us through binoculars, and sweeping the sky in Ursa Minor will bring out many pretty pairs. A small telescope will show the 5th and 6th magnitude stars forming the double star Psi Draconis, while binoculars will reveal the two 5th magnitude components of Kuma, the faintest of the four stars which form the head of the constellation Draco.

Left: *A portion of the night sky that shows the famous constellation Ursa Minor. The leading star Polaris lies very close to the point in the sky known as the North Celestial Pole and is visible at the upper right corner of the photograph. Its brightness and position made it a guiding light for early navigators and explorers.*

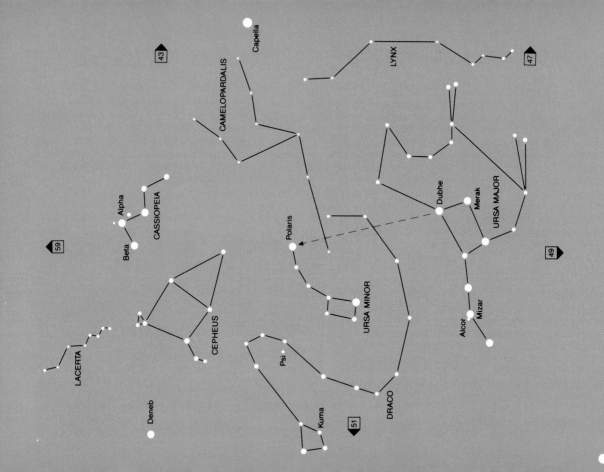

THE ORION TO ERIDANUS REGION

Visible during the northern winter/southern summer, this region of sky includes several distinctive constellations. Named after the hunter of Greek legend, Orion is one of the most famous and well-known groups in the entire sky. To the south of Orion is Lepus (The Hare) and the constellation Eridanus (The River Eridanus) which winds it way down from Orion towards southern skies. North-west of Orion is Taurus (The Bull), the three stars in Orion's Belt pointing the way to its leading star Aldebaran. To the north of Taurus is the inverted 'Y' of Perseus and the prominent circlet of stars forming Auriga (The Charioteer). Also on our chart are Triangulum (The Triangle) and Aries (The Ram), together with the eastern region of Cetus (The Whale). Two more dim groups round off the chart, these being Columba (The Dove) and Caelum (The Graving Tool), both located to the south of Lepus.

The Pleiades

A showpiece of Taurus is the open cluster M45, also known as The Pleiades. This magnificent formation contains around 500 stars and is thought to be around 60 million years old. The regions between its member stars contain dust and gas which are traces of the original nebula from which the stars in The Pleiades were formed. It lies at a distance of 420 light years and is best viewed through binoculars which will allow you to see the complete cluster at one go.

Right: *The magnificent Orion with the older Hyades open cluster of stars to the upper right of the picture beyond Aldebaran.*

Variable Stars

Variable stars are stars whose brightness changes over periods of time. Of the many different types of variable star there are two main ones: *intrinsic* variables which vary due to changes taking place within the star itself; and *extrinsic* variables which vary because of the effects of another object. This chart contains two of the most famous examples: Algol in Perseus and Mira in Cetus.

Algol is an extrinsic variable of the type known as an eclipsing binary. In reality it is a binary star system, one member of which is much fainter than the other. The two stars orbit

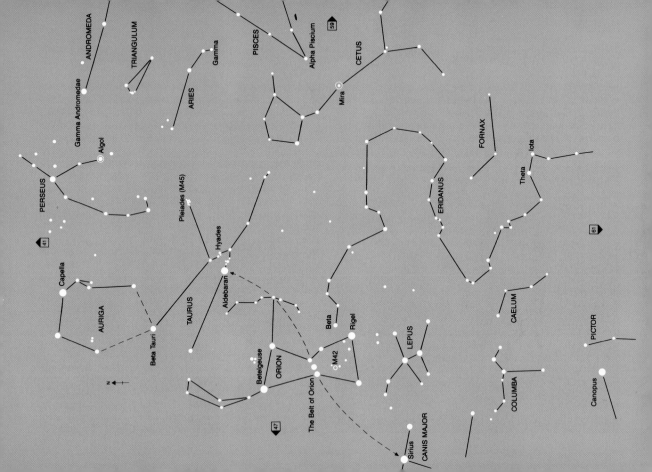

each other every 2.867 days and, because their orbital plane is almost exactly aligned with the Earth's position in space, the fainter companion regularly passes in front of, or eclipses, its brighter companion. When this happens, the overall light output of the system drops. In the case of Algol, the magnitude decreases from 2.1 to 3.4 before increasing again. Predic-

tions for Algol are given in many astronomical magazines and periodicals and the variations can be followed by comparing Algol's brightness relative to other nearby stars.

Mira is a long-period variable. Intrinsic variables of this type are the most common known. They are all red giant stars and some 4,000 have been catalogued. The changes in the light output of long-period variables are caused by pulsations within the stars themselves which make them expand and contract. Although Mira's period of variability is not regular it averages out to around 331 days, the magnitude fluctuating between around 3 and 9. Binoculars or a small telescope will allow you to follow the complete cycle. Locate Mira by using the chart, bearing in mind that should you have difficulty in picking it out the star may be at or near its minimum magnitude. In this case, keep an eye on the area until it comes back into view. As is the case for Algol, predictions for Mira appear in a number of publications.

Nebulae
Nebulae are interstellar clouds of dust and gas. Many nebulae have been catalogued both within our own Galaxy and other galaxies. There are three basic types of nebula: *emission* nebulae have a characteristic red colour and shine because they contain very hot stars. The vast amounts of ultraviolet energy emitted by these stars is absorbed by the surround-

Left: *M43 (NGC 1977) is an emission nebula at the northern end of the Orion Nebula. The bright stars are 42 and 45 Orionis.*

ing nebulosity which in turn emits visible light. *Reflection* nebulae contains no stars hot enough to cause the gas within the nebula to glow and only shine by reflecting the light from nearby stars; *dark* nebulae, such as The Coalsack (see page 62), contain no stars whatsoever and take the appearance of dark patches superimposed against the stellar background.

Orion

Orion is a distinctive group whose two main stars are Betelgeuse and Rigel. Betelgeuse is a red giant star marking Orion's shoulder; its name is derived from the Arabic for "Armpit of the Central One". Betelgeuse is actually variable, although the variations are difficult to observe, because they are only slight and take place over a period approaching six years — long by Earth's standards.

The blue-white supergiant Rigel has a diameter of around 50 times that of the Sun and is a truly brilliant star. Its actual luminosity is around 60,000 times that of our parent star. Rigel has a faint companion star of magnitude 6.7 although its feeble glow, easily swamped by Rigel's brilliance, can only be detected in large telescopes.

The Orion Nebula (M42) is an emission nebula. Shining from a distance of 1,600 light years, M42 is located just south of the three stars forming Orion's Belt. This huge cloud of glowing gas is clearly visible to the naked eye as a shimmering patch of light. The energy which causes the gas within the Orion Nebula to shine comes from the multiple star Theta Orionis which is embedded deep within the nebula.

Right: *The Orion Nebula (M42) is a region where glowing gas and young, hot stars mingle with cool, dense clouds of dust.*

THE LYNX TO PUPPIS REGION

This region of sky is visible during the evenings in northern spring/southern autumn and includes a number of bright, easily distinguished constellations. The striking star patterns of Orion lie just to the north of Lepus (The Hare). Really clear skies allow the faint Monoceros (The Unicorn) to be traced out to the east of Orion. Monoceros is flanked by Canis Minor (The Little Dog) to its north and Canis Major (The Great Dog) to the south, the latter highlighted by its leading star Sirius.

The bright stars Capella in Auriga (The Charioteer), Castor and Pollux in Gemini (The Twins) and Regulus in Leo (The Lion) span the northern section of the chart. They are accompanied by the line of stars forming Lynx (The Lynx). The legendary journey of Jason and the Argonauts in search of the Golden Fleece is represented by constellations towards the south. This area of sky was originally occupied by Argo Navis, a huge and unwieldly group which was turned into the four constellations of Vela (The Sails), Carina (The Keel), Puppis (The Poop) and Pyxis (The Mariner's Compass).

Spanning the border between Vela and Carina, and formed from two bright stars in each constellation, is the "False Cross". Care should be taken not to confuse this striking pattern with the constellation Crux (The Cross) which lies nearby and is shown on the South Circumpolar chart on page 61. Other groups seen here are Sextans (The Sextant), just to the north of the western end of Hydra (The Water Snake); Antlia (The Air Pump), further to the south; while to the west of Puppis are the small groups Columba (The Dove) and Caelum (The Graving Tool).

Gemini and Cancer
Gemini is a prominent group, well indicated by its leading stars Castor and Pollux. Gemini contains the bright open cluster M35 which is found just to the east of the star 1 Geminorum. You can actually glimpse M35 with the naked eye if the sky is really dark and clear. The cluster lies at a distance of around 2,200 light years. It is quite large and binoculars are good for observing the group.

To the south-east of Gemini is the faint constellation of Cancer (The Crab) whose main objects of interest are the open clusters M44 and M67. Also known as Praesepe, or The Beehive, M44 has a magnitude of 3.1 and can be seen with the naked eye. It is best observed through large binoculars or a wide-field telescope as it covers an area of sky over twice the diameter of a full Moon. M44 lies at a distance of around 520 light years and contains some 350 stars.

Right: *The spiral galaxy M83 is also called the Southern Pinwheel. It lies at a distance of some 10 million light years in the largest single constellation of Hydra. It is about 30,000 light years across.*

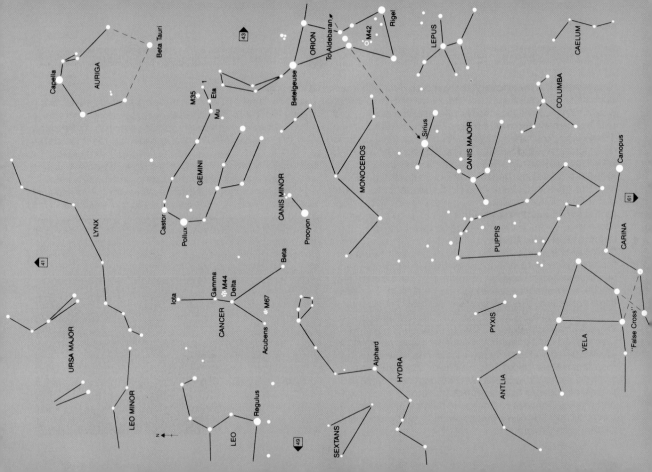

THE LEO, VIRGO AND HYDRA REGIONS

Here we see the evening sky as it appears during the northern spring/southern autumn. The curve of The Plough's handle (Big Dipper) leads the way first to Arcturus in Bootes (The Herdsman) and then Spica in Virgo (The Virgin). Leo (The Lion) is accompanied by Leo Minor (The Little Lion) and other small groups include Canes Venatici (The Hunting Dogs), located just below The Plough's handle, and the rather faint Coma Berenices (Berenice's Hair). South of Virgo is Corvus (The Crow) and Crater (The Cup), the winding shape of Hydra (The Water Snake) running underneath. Antlia (The Air Pump) rounds off the chart.

Mel 111 Open Star Cluster

The open star cluster Mel 111 contains around 40 stars and lies at a distance of 250 light years. Also knownas the Coma Star Cluster, Mel 111 has an overall magnitude of about 3 and is easily seen with the naked eye on clear nights. Its apparently large size means that it is best viewed through binoculars.

Virgo's Sombrero Hat

Glowing at 8th magnitude, the edge-on spiral galaxy M104 (NGC4594) can be seen through binoculars if the sky is really dark and clear. Using the stars Psi and Chi Virginis as a guide the area of sky just to the south should be swept carefully. M104 can be seen through almost any telescope, with larger instruments, needless to say, giving the best views. M104 is around 40 million light years away and has a diameter of about 130,000 light years.

R Hydrae

To the south-east of Corvus is the trio of stars called Psi, Gamma and R Hydrae. The latter is a long period variable whose magnitude varies between 4 and 10 over a period of 386 days. A small telescope will allow you to follow its cycle of variability.

Below: *The overall appearance of the spiral galaxy M104 has led to its name of Sombrero. The huge nuclear bulge contains many old, red stars while the dark band around it is formed from heavy dust clouds. The blue halo is the light of faint stars.*

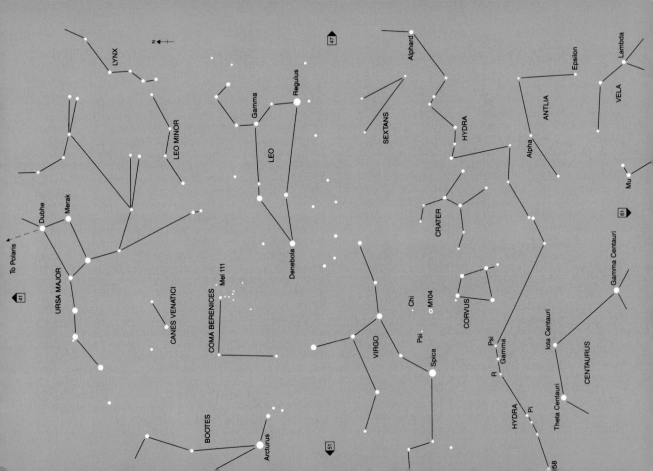

THE HERCULES TO SCORPIUS REGION

This chart is centred on the sprawling constellation of Ophiuchus (The Serpent Bearer) who, true to his description, is firmly holding Serpens Caput and Serpens Cauda (Head and Tail of the Serpent). Further to the north we see Hercules, a group depicting the legendary hero famed for his twelve labours. Hercules is flanked by Corona Borealis (The Northern Crown) and Lyra (The Lyre). Near the southern end of the chart we see Scorpius (The Scorpion) with the unmistakable curve of its tail. Libra (The Scales) and the distinctive shape of Lupus (The Wolf) adjoin Scorpius, while to the east of The Scorpion are some stars in the constellation Sagittarius (The Archer).

Star Clusters

Many stars are members of collections known as star clusters. There are two basic types of star cluster, *open* and *globular*, and each has its own basic characteristics.

Also known as galactic clusters, open clusters are found along the plane of The Milky Way. They orbit the centre of our Galaxy in paths which are more or less circular. They can contain anything fom a dozen to several hundred stars and can be up to several tens of light years across. They have no regular, well-defined shape and contain stars which are much younger than those found within globulars.

Globular clusters, as their name suggests, are huge spherical gatherings of older stars. With diameters ranging from a few tens to several hundred light years, they can contain many thousands of individual stars. They are found outside the main plane of our Galaxy, orbiting the galactic centre in huge, eccentric paths. The stars within globulars are relatively tightly packed, particularly towards the centre of the cluster. This leads to a combined gravitational pull which helps the cluster retain its uniform, spherical shape.

There are many star clusters within the light grasp of binoculars or small telescopes, including several within the boundaries of Hercules and Scorpius.

Left: *The huge elliptical galaxy NGC 5128 in Centaurus is one of the largest and most luminous known. An impressive sight optically, it is also a strong source of radio and X-ray radiation. The dark band may be a spiral galaxy merging with it.*

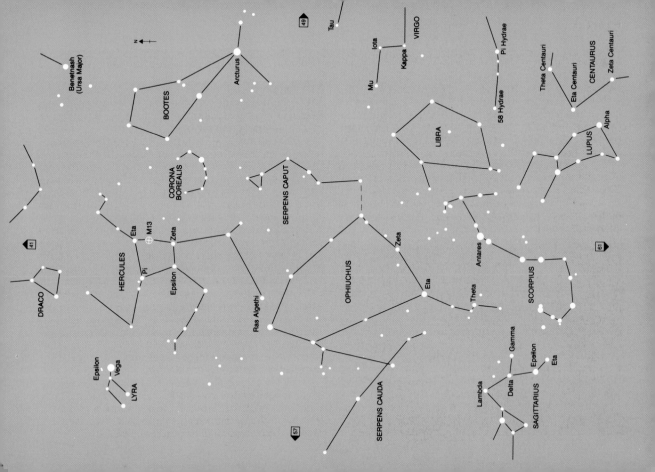

THE HERCULES TO SCORPIUS REGION

Hercules

Hercules is a large but somewhat faint constellation, although its so-called "Keystone", which is made up of the four stars Eta, Zeta, Epsilon and Pi Herculis, is quite distinctive. A line from the brilliant Arcturus through the conspicuous circlet of Corona Borealis will lead you to The Keystone.

Hercules plays host to one of the most famous globular clusters in the entire sky: M13 (NGC6205), also known as the Great Hercules Cluster. It lies at a distance of over 20,000 light years and has a diameter of around 200 light years. At magnitude 5.9 it can be glimpsed with the naked eye if the sky is really dark and clear. It is located approximately a third of the way from Eta to Zeta Herculis. Binoculars will show M13 as a fuzzy patch of light while moderate telescopes will bring out one or two of its outlying stars.

Ras Algethi (Alpha Herculis) is a variable star whose magnitude ranges from 3.1 to 3.9 over a period of around 100 days. The variability is irregular and may be difficult to spot. Less of a challenge is its companion star of magnitude 5.39 which can be seen in small telescopes.

Scorpius

The leading star of Scorpius is Antares, a magnitude 0.92 supergiant star whose name means "Rival of Mars". This derives from the fact that when Mars is in the region of Antares the prominent ruddy glow of Antares rivals that of the Red Planet. The actual luminosity of this colossal star is around 9,000 times that of our own Sun, yet its distance of

Above: *The great globular cluster M13 in Hercules is the finest object of its type in the northern sky and has perhaps 300,000 stars. There are over 100 globular clusters in our Galaxy alone.*

520 light years demotes it to the position of 15th brightest star in the sky.

Small telescopes will reveal the magnitude 2.6 and 4.9 white components of the double star Beta Scorpii. Further to the south the two stars Zeta$_1$ and Zeta$_2$ Scorpii form a naked-eye double. Binoculars may bring out the orange tint of Zeta$_1$ and the bluish hue of Zeta$_2$.

Left: *The brilliant region of Scorpius contains the nebula around the star Rho Ophiuchi (top right), the globular star cluster nearest the Sun — M4 (top centre), plus the red supergiant star Antares (centre left).*

Right: *Over 1° across, open cluster M7 can be seen with the naked eye.*

Scorpius contains a number of open star clusters within the light grasp of binoculars. Of particular interest are M6 (NGC6405) and M7 (NGC6475) which are found just to the east of The Scorpion's sting. Magnitude 4.6 M6 contains around 130 stars shining from a distance of 1,200 light years. It can be seen with the naked eye, as can 3rd magnitude M7. This fine object is somewhat nearer than M6, lying at a distance of 800 light years.

The globular cluster M4 (NGC6121) is found just to the west of Antares. It is a fine object for small telescopes which will resolve some of its member stars. M4 lies at a distance of around 18,000 light years and, at 6th magnitude, can easily be picked up in binoculars. Its position relative to Antares ensures ease of location!

THE SUMMER TRIANGLE

This chart shows the area of sky centred on the three bright stars which form the Summer Triangle. Deneb, marking the tail of Cygnus (The Swan), shines at a magnitude of 1.26 from a distance of 1,600 light years.Vega (magnitude 0.04), in Lyra (The Lyre), is much nearer, lying at a distance of 27 light years. Closer still is Altair (magnitude 0.77) in Aquila (The Eagle) which marks the southern corner of the Summer Triangle; it lies at a distance of just 16 light years.

Other groups on the chart include the tiny but conspicuous Delphinus (The Dolphin) and Sagitta (The Arrow). Harder to pick out are Vulpecula (The Fox) and Equuleus (The Foal). Scutum (The Shield) can be seen just to the south-west of Aquila. The Milky Way passes through Cygnus, Sagitta, Aquila and Scutum and sweeping this area of sky with binoculars will reveal many faint stars.

The prettiest double star in this area is Albireo in Cygnus. The 3rd and 5th magnitude yellow and blue stars forming Albireo are viewed easily through a small telescope, as are the yellowish and greenish 5th and 6th magnitude stars of Gamma Delphini. The most famous double on this chart is Epsilon Lyrae, the "Double-Double" located close to Vega. Binoculars (or keen eyesight) will show that Epsilon is a double and telescopes will reveal that each of the two main 5th magnitude components is double again.

Star Clusters

M39 (NGC7092) in Cygnus is a fine example of an open cluster. It can be found to the north-east of Deneb by using the chart. Lying at a distance of around 800 light years, this pretty cluster is easily spotted through binoculars which will resolve several of its 30 or so member stars. Binoculars will also reveal the distinctive wedge-shape appearance of this cluster. M26 (NGC6694) in Scutum is described on page 56.

The stars forming the globular cluster M56 (NGC6779), lying roughly midway between Gamma Lyrae and Albireo, shine with an overall magnitude of 8.2. M56 lies some 46,000 light years away and can be seen as a fuzzy, spherical patch of light when viewed through good binoculars or a small telescope. Larger telescopes will bring out a number of individual stars around its outer edges.

Above: *M56 is an 8th magnitude globular cluster located near the border between the constellations of Cygnus and Lyra.*

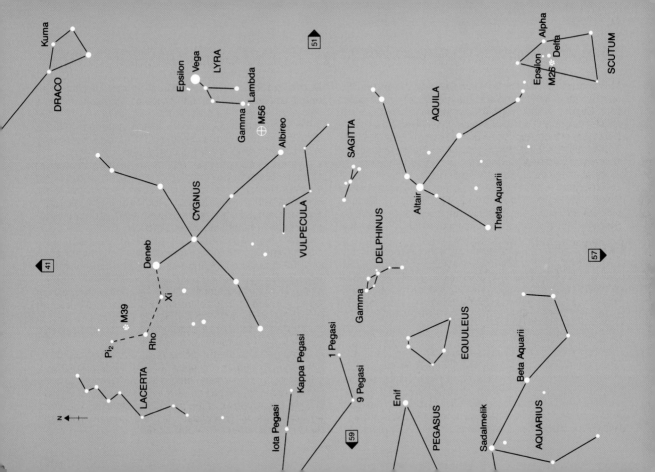

THE CAPRICORNUS TO SAGITTARIUS REGION

The main groups on this chart are Sagittarius and Capricornus, this area of sky being observable during northern summer/southern winter evenings. To the east of Sagittarius is the dim constellation Microscopium (The Microscope), while the prominent circlet of stars forming Corona Australis (The Southern Crown) lies just to the south. Another optical instrument is depicted by the undistinguished group Telescopium (The Telescope), while Indus (The Indian) is equally obscure. Much more prominent is the conspicuous shape of Grus (The Crane), found immediately to the southwest of Piscis Austrinus (The Southern Fish). Piscis Austrinus' main claim to fame is the star Fomalhaut, which is also known as the "The Solitary One". It derives its title from the fact that there are no other conspicuous stars in the surrounding sky.

The constellations shown lie to the south of those depicted on page 55, the constellation Scutum being included on both charts. From Scutum, the Milky Way passes through Sagittarius and many rich star fields are visible in this region. Time spent looking with binoculars will be well rewarded.

Doubles in Capricornus

Capricornus contains the double star Alpha Capricorni. The two main components, $Alpha_1$ and $Alpha_2$, have magnitudes of 4.2 and 3.6 and are so far apart that they can be separated with the naked eye. The two stars form an optical double and are not physically related to each other. $Alpha_1$ shines from a distance of almost 500 light years, while $Alpha_2$ is only 36 light years away. Closer examination with a telescope will show that each of these stars is double again; $Alpha_1$ is an optical double with a faint 9th magnitude companion, while $Alpha_2$ is a binary the other component of which shines at magnitude 10.6. Beta Capricorni is another wide double whose components (magnitudes 3.4 and 6.2) are travelling through space together.

Open Clusters in Scutum

Visible inside the quadrilateral of stars forming Scutum is the open cluster M26 which lies at a distance of nearly 5,000 light years. Small telescopes will reveal around a dozen of the 30 or so members of this compact little group. Also visible in the same area is NGC6664, a collection of around 50 stars shining with a combined magnitude of 7.8 from a distance of 4,000 light years.

Left: *Also known as the Horseshoe or Swan Nebula, the Omega Nebula (M17) is not on the chart but can be found 6,000 light years away to the south-west of Scutum. Its overall length is about 40 light years.*

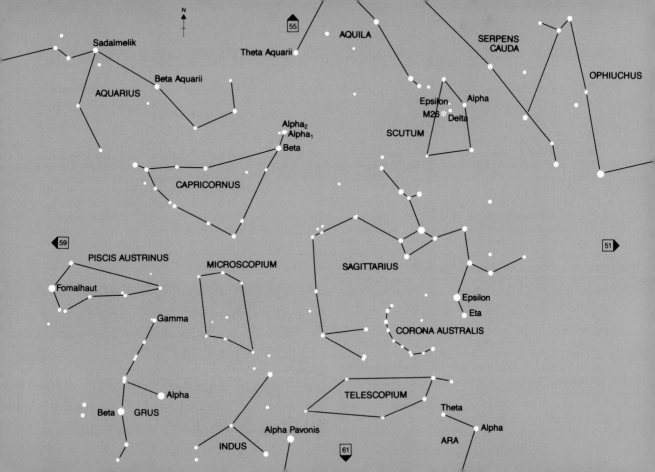

THE PEGASUS TO PISCIS AUSTRINUS REGION

The evening sky of northern autumn/southern spring is dominated for northern hemisphere observers by Pegasus, the winged horse from Greek legend. The "Square of Pegasus" is formed from Markab (Alpha Pegasi), Scheat (Beta Pegasi), Algenib (Gamma Pegasi) and Alpheratz (Alpha Andromedae), the latter "borrowed" from neighbouring Andromeda. Given clear skies a dozen or so stars can be seen with the naked eye within the Square of Pegasus. How many can you count?

Andromeda, named after the legendary princess, is accompanied by Triangulum (The Triangle) and Aries (The Ram). Pisces (The Fishes) extends around the south-eastern corner of Pegasus. South of Pisces is part of Cetus (The Whale) with Aquarius (The Water Carrier) to the west. A line from Scheat through Markab in Pegasus exended to the south will lead to the bright star Fomalhaut in Piscis Austrinus (The Southern Fish); to the east of this is the faint constellation Sculptor (The Sculptor).

Andromeda
Also know as the Andromeda Galaxy, M31 (NGC224) can be tracked down by following the line of stars Beta, Mu and Nu Andromedae to where it is situated immediately to the west of Nu. Located 2.2 million light years away, this huge spiral galaxy contains around 300,000 million stars and shines with an overall magnitude of 3.5. M31 can be seen with the naked eye as a misty streak of light. Binoculars reveal its bright core, with the spiral arms visible as fainter nebulous regions reaching out to either side of the core. M31 has a diameter of around 180,000 light years, making it roughly half as large again as our own Milky Way Galaxy.

Double Stars
Small telescopes will resolve the 2nd and 5th magnitude yellowish-orange and bluish components of Gamma Andromedae, one of the prettiest doubles in the entire sky. Another impressive sight is presented by the two bluish-white components of Gamma Arietis (magnitude 4.8), while further to the south we have Beta Piscis Austrini which is comprised of magnitude 4.4 and 7.9 stars.

Below: *The edge-on spiral galaxy NGC 55 is an 8th magnitude member of the nearby constellation Sculptor's group of galaxies.*

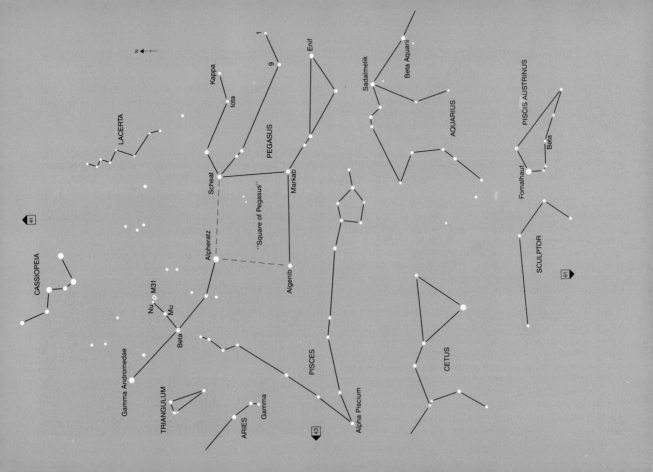

THE SOUTH CIRCUMPOLAR STARS

The region of sky surrounding the South Celestial Pole is occupied by a number of faint constellations. Groups like Dorado (The Goldfish), Hydrus (The Little Water Snake) and Volans (The Flying Fish) will test your powers of detection on all but the clearest of nights. The Pole itself is located within the constellation Octans (The Octant) and lies more or less on a line between Acrux in Crux and Achernar which marks the end of the long and winding constellation Eridanus (The River Eridanus). Unlike its northern counterpart there is, unfortunately, no really conspicuous star marking the position of the South Celestial Pole.

Many groups in this region reflect the fact that they were only mapped by astronomers during the last couple of centuries or so. Unlike the classical constellation names of northern skies, such as Orion and Hercules, we see such unromantically-named groups as Telescopium (The Telescope), Microscopium (The Microscope) and Horologium (The Pendulum Clock)!

Notable objects in this region of sky include two galaxies which lie quite close to our own Milky Way. These are the Large and Small Magellanic Clouds, named in honour of the explorer Ferdinand Magellan in view of the fact that they were discovered during one of his voyages through the south seas. Both objects can be found by using the bright star Achernar as a starting point. The Large Magellanic Cloud (LMC) is located on the borders of Dorado and Mensa, while the Small Magellanic Cloud (SMC) lies on the edge of the triangle of stars forming Hydrus. The SMC is situated around 200,000 light years away, the LMC being somewhat nearer at 180,000 light years. At first sight they take on the appearance of detached sections of the Milky Way, although closer observation reveals them to be galaxies in their own right.

Below: *A galaxy in its own right the Large Magellanic Cloud is seen here behind the stars of our Milky Way. It may have some 10,000 million stars — less than 10 per cent of our total.*

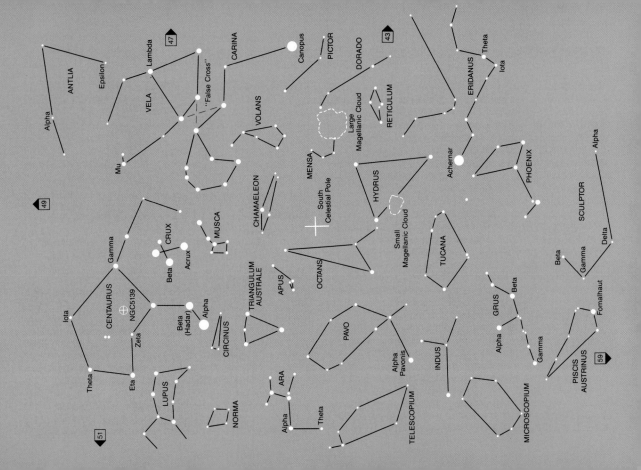

THE SOUTH CIRCUMPOLAR STARS

Galaxies

Galaxies are huge collections of billions of stars, clusters, nebulae and other interstellar material. There are several basic types, including irregular galaxies (of which the LMC and SMC are both examples) which have no clear or well-defined shape. By contrast, spiral galaxies, as their name suggests, contain spiral arms radiating out from a central bulge and are further classified according to the sizes of their central bulge and how tightly wound their spiral arms are. Our Milky Way is a colossal spiral system with over 100 billion stars. Its pearly glow is made up from the light of the stars along the main plane of our Galaxy. It is thought to have a diameter of 100,000 light years. Another type of galaxy are barred spirals, the spiral arms of which emerge from the ends of a bar which crosses the central regions of the galaxy.

Elliptical galaxies are the most numerous type and consist of huge symmetrical gatherings of stars. Ellipticals contain little if any interstellar material, unlike the spirals whose arms play host to huge amounts of dust and gas. Elliptical galaxies are further classified according to their overall shape, ranging from highly elongated to almost spherical; examples of the latter resemble huge globular clusters.

Galaxies are generally found in clusters and our own Milky Way is no exception. Together with the Magellanic Clouds and over 20 other galaxies it is a member of the Local Group of Galaxies. Other clusters, of which many examples are seen scattered throughout the universe, may contain well over a thousand individual galaxies within their ranks.

Above: *The Small Magellanic Cloud contains the usual nebulae and star ingredients of galaxies. Note the red globular clusters.*

Crux and Musca

The small but conspicuous constellations of Crux (The Cross) and Musca (The Fly) contain several notable objects, including the bright open cluster NGC 4755 which is also known as The Jewel Box. Even binoculars will show many individual stars within this cluster which lies at a distance of around 7,500 light years. Also in Crux is The Coalsack dark nebula, a huge cloud of dust which contains no stars and which blots out the light from the stars beyond it. The Coalsack lies at a distance of around 500 light years and, like other dark nebulae, takes on the appearance of a huge hole in the sky.

Nearby Musca is easily picked out because its main stars form a conspicuous pattern. Lying against a pretty backdrop

Left: *With a larger area than a full Moon the globular cluster Omega Centauri is widely regarded as the best in the heavens.*

Right: *The open cluster known as The Jewel Box lies quite close to Beta Crucis. A stunning sight, it contains a number of bright stars lending it blue and red tints.*

of stars, the double star Theta Muscae is easily resolvable in small telescopes. It is made up of magnitude 5.7 and 7.3 yellow and white companions.

Lying close to Crux and Musca are the two stars Alpha and Beta Centauri. Alpha Centauri is the closest of the bright stars, shining from a distance of just 4.34 light years. Alpha is a triple star system, its two main components forming a binary star with yellow magnitude 0.0 and 1.2 stars orbiting each other every 80 years. Although the distance between them varies over the orbital period both stars are currently resolvable with small telescopes.

The third member of the Alpha Centauri system is Proxima Centauri (magnitude 10.7) which holds the distinction of being the star closest to Earth. This dim red dwarf is currently at a distance of just 4.3 light years and its feeble glow (Proxima Centauri's actual luminosity is just 1/13,000 that of the Sun) is only detectable with larger telescopes. Also in Centaurus, and shown on the main chart, is the prominent globular cluster Omega Centauri or NGC 5139. This colossal ball of stars occupies an area of sky roughly the size of the Moon, and even binoculars will resolve some of its members. Originally thought to be a star (hence its name Omega Centauri), its true identity as a globular cluster was discovered in 1677 by the English astronomer Edmund Halley. Omega Centauri is considered to be the best example of a globular cluster in the entire sky.

Index

Page references set in *Italic* type refer to subjects in illustrations

A
Acrux 38
Adams, John Couch 21
Albireo 54
Algol 42, 44
Alpha Centauri 63
Altair 54
Andromeda 58
Andromeda Galaxy 58
Antares 31, 52, *53*
Aurorae 11, 28-29, *28, 29*

B
Bayer, Johann 38
Beta Centauri 63
Betelgeuse 38, 45
Biot, Jean Baptiste 27
Black dwarfs 32
Black holes 33
Brahe, Tycho 7

C
Caelum 38
Callisto 18
Caloris Basin *14*
Cancer 46
Canopus 36
Capricornus 56
Cassini, Giovanni 18
Castor 38, 46
Celestial poles 34-35
  38, 40, 60
Celestial Sphere 34-35
Centaurus 50

Ceres 17
Charon 23, *23*
Christy, James W 23
Coalsack Nebula 38 *39*,
  45, 62
Comets 24-25, *24, 25*,
  26, 39
Constellations 34-35
  charts 38, 40-61
Copernicus, Nicolas 6, *7*
Crab Nebula *32*
Crux 38, *39*, 46, 62-63
Cygnus X-1 33

D
Deimos 16
Deneb 54
Dione 19
Dreyer, J L E 39
Dubhe 36, 37

E
Earth 8, *8*
Eclipses,
  lunar 13
  solar 6, *10*, 11, *11*
Encke's Comet 24
Epsilon Lyrae 54
Eridanus 38
Europa 18

F
False Cross 46
Fireballs 26
Fomalhaut 56
Fornax 38

G
Galaxies 62
Galilei, Galileo 7, *7*, 18
Gamma Delphini 54
Ganymede 18

Gegenschein 29
Gemini 38, 46

H
Halley's Comet 24, 25, *25*
Halley, Edmund 25, 63
HDE 226868 (star) 33
Hercules 50, 52
Herschel, William 20
Horologium 34, 38
Huygens, Christiaan 19
Hyades *42*

I
Iapetus 19
Io 18
IRAS 7, *7*

J
Jewel Box 62, *63*
Jupiter 8, *8*, 17, 18, *18*, 20

K
Kepler, Johannes 6, 7
Kuma 40

L
Large Magellanic Cloud
  33, 60, *60*, 62
Lepus 38
Leverrier, Urbain Jean
  Joseph 21
Light year 36
Local Group 62
Lowell, Percival 22, 23

M
M4 *53*
M6 53
M7 53, *53*
M13 *52*
M17 *56*

M26 56
M31 58
M35 46
M39 54
M43 *44*
M44 46
M56 54, *54*
M67 46
M83 *46*
M104 *48*
Magnitudes 36
Marius, Simon 18
Mars 8, *8*, 16-17, *16*, 52
Mel 111 (cluster) 48
Merak 36, 37
Mercury 14, *14*
Messier, Charles 39
Meteorites 12, 27, *27*
Meteoroids 26
Meteors 25, 26-27, *26*
Milky Way 7, 38, 50, 56,
  60, *60*, 62
Minor planets 17, 27
Mira 42, 44
Miranda 20, 21
Moon 12-13, *12, 13*, 27, 37
Musca 62-63

N
Nebulae 30, 44-45
Neptune 8, *8, 20*, 21,
  22, 23
Neutron stars 32-33
NGC55 *58*
NGC3132 *32*
NGC5128 *50*
NGC6664 56
NGC7538 *31*

O
Octans 40
Omega Centauri 63, *63*

Omega Nebula 56
Oort's Cloud 24
Ophiuchus 27
Orion *26*, 38, 42, *42*, 45
Orion Nebula 39, 45, *45*

P
Pegasus 58
Perseus 27
Phobos 16
Planetary nebulae 32, 33
Planets 8-9 (see
  individual entries)
Pleiades *30*, 42
Plough 36, 37, 40
Pluto 22-23, *22, 23*
Polaris *34*, 40
Pollux 38, 46
Praesepe 46
Protostars 30
Proxima Centauri 63
Ptolemy 6
Pulsars 33

R
R Hydrae 48
Ras Algethi 52
Red giants 30, 32
Rhea 19
Rho Ophiuchi *53*
Rigel *26*, 45

S
Saturn 8, *8*, 18-19, *19*, 20
Schiaparelli, Giovanni 16
Scorpius 31, 50, 52-53
Scutum 56
Sigma Octantis 40
Sirius 36
Small Magellanic Cloud
  60, 62, *62*
Solar System *8*, 8-9, 36

Solar wind 11, 24, 28
Star clusters 50
Stars 30-62
  brightest (table) 36
  distances 36
  double/binary 40, 33
  evolution 30-33
  names 38
  nearest (table) 36
  variable 42-44
Summer Triangle 54
Sun *8, 9*, 10-11, 24, 31
Supernovae 32-33, *33*
Swift-Tuttle, Comet 27

T
Taurus 32
Telescope 7
Telescopium 34
Tethys 19
Thales of Miletus 6
Titan 19
Tombaugh, Clyde 22, 23
Triton 21, *21*

U
Uranus 20-21, *20*
Ursa Major 40
Ursa Minor *40*

V
Valles Marineris *17*
Van Allen Belts 28
Vega 54
Vela 32, 46
Venus 8, *8*, 14, 15, *15*

W
White Dwarfs 32

Z
Zodiacal Light 29